Where The Trent Rises

For Barbara, Oscar and Blake

Where The Trent Rises

John Lancaster

Clayhanger Press | Newcastle-under-Lyme

2023

This book or any portion thereof may not be reproduced or used in any manner whatsoever without the express written permission of the copyright holder except for the use of brief quotations in a book review.

The right of John Lancaster to be identified as the author of this work has been asserted by him in accordance with the Copyright, Design and Patents Act 1988.

Typeset in Times New Roman

First Printing 2023

Published by Clayhanger Press
7 Highfield Court
Newcastle under Lyme
Staffordshire
ST5 3LT
www.clayhangerpress.co.uk

All rights reserved.

ISBN-13: 978-1-7391770-5-8

Acknowledgements

The following poems or versions of them have been published in magazines, anthologies or online websites or won prizes or listings in poetry competitions and thanks are due to all the editors, judges and organizers concerned:
A Thank You To Biddulph Library: The Alchemy Spoon, Issue 8, Winter 2022. *The Half-A-Crown*: Live Canon 2022 Anthology, shortlisted Live Canon International Poetry Prize. *The Home Game* and *Coming Home For The Funeral*: The North, Vol. 66, Aug. 2021. *What Might Have Been*: The Frogmore Papers, No. 102, 2023.
The Island Surveyor: commended Ver Poets Open Poetry Competition 2021, published in the prize winner's anthology. *The Search*: shortlisted for the Ver Prize in 2020, published in the competition anthology. *Still Cutting It*: Bracken (US) Vol.VI, Dec. 2018. *Baldwin's Iron And Steelworks, Swindon*: anthologised in The Poetry of the Black Country, Offa's Press 2017. *Sex Education At Boots*: MONO blog, Nov. 2022. *The Wedding Speech*, third prize, and *Laughter Lines For Hanley High*, commended, Fire River Poets Competition, 2016, and both published online. *Is There Anything You Would Like To Ask Us?*: Ta DADA, the 6ress, No. 4 Jan. 2023. *At Biddulph Wakes*: The Wide Skirt, No. 30, 1997. *Sussed: Cobridge 1974* as *Sussed,* runner-up, The Frogmore Poetry Prize 2022, published in The Frogmore Papers, No. 100, Autumn 2022. *Anniversary*: The Echo Room No. 12, 1989. *Case Notes (as Mr Cahill and Mr Jones)*: longlisted for the Yeovil Poetry Prize, 2020. *Going Home I.* as *Things You Could Have Said*: Iron No. 54, 1988. *Oranges* and *What Did You Do Today?*: The Wide Skirt No. 30, 1987.
From the sequence *Into A Green Unpleasant Land*, twelve poems have been published: *What Justice In This Green Unpleasant Land*; *The Black Lad*; *Miss Fairey; Stan; Jim Shuff; Doctor Curry*; *Cousin Rosemary I. and III.* : The North, Vol. 60, August 2018. *The Locum*: shortlisted Wells Poetry Prize, published in Wells Festival of Literature Poetry Competition Anthology 2019. *The Egg Boy I.* as *Rom.VII.23*: winner Poetry Society Poetry News Competition, published Poetry News, December 2020 and online video at Poetry Society Members' Poems. *The Egg Boy II.* as *The Swing*: McLellan Poetry Competition 2016, commended prizewinner and published online. *Sam* as *Up Stony Lane*: Under The Radar, No. 31, 2023. The sequence *Into A Green Unpleasant Land* was also longlisted for the Overton Prize Poetry Competition 2017.
The nineteen-poem sequence *Potters: A Division Of Labour* was published as a book/pamphlet, Longmarsh Press, 2017 and won the inaugural Arnold Bennett Book Prize, 2017. Six of the poems *Rex, The Dish Maker*; *Chris, The Plate Maker*; *Doris, The Cup Handler*; *Terry, The Mould Runner*; *Hilda, The Fettler*; *Frank, The Manager* were previously published in Encounter, 1985 and the collection *Effects Of War*, Giant Steps Press, 1986 and broadcast on BBC Radio Stoke. A further seven poems, *Barry, The Clay Carrier*; *Johnny, The Placer*; *Beryl, The Decorator*; *Dick, The Mould Maker*; *John, The Student*; *Brian, The Union Man* were published in The North, Vol. 57, 2017. *Dennis, The Slip Caster* (*as The Slip Caster of Stoke*) was anthologised in Places of Poetry, Oneworld Publications, October 2020 and pinned on Places of Poetry online map.

Contents

Part I. On Biddulph Moor	9
I. What Justice In This Green Unpleasant Land?	10
II. And What Justice For Them	11
The Egg Boy I.	12
II.	13
Bobby Cole	14
Roy	15
Bould	16
The Black Lad	17
Maeve	18
Dirty Danny	19
Miss Fairey	20
The Locum	21
Stan	22
Sam	23
Beech	24
Jim Shuff	25
Doctor Curry	26
The Browns: I. The Landlord	27
II. Nell	28
Cousin Rosemary I.	29
II.	30
III.	31
IV.	32
Glossary	33
Part II. Hereabouts and Thereabouts	34
A Thank You To Biddulph Library	35
The Half-A-Crown	36
Laughter Lines for Hanley High	37
Coming Home For The Funeral	38
What Might Have Been	39

In The 1930s: I. Them and Us and The Holditch Colliery Disaster	40
II. A Short History Of The Great Depression	41
A Wesleyan Sunday School Outing	43
At Biddulph Wakes	44
Sussed: Cobridge 1974	45
Still Cutting It	46
Is There Anything You Would Like To Ask Us?	47
The Home Game	48
Channel-Hopping With The Barman	49
The Island Surveyor	50
Sex Education at Boots	51
Baldwin's Iron and Steelworks, Swindon	52
The Search	53
Anniversary	54
The Wedding Speech	55
Case Notes	56
From Kumasi to Kidsgrove	57
Oranges	62
What Did You Do Today?	63
Going Home I.	65
II.	66
Henry Whiston	67
I Crave A Listener For This	68
Part III. Potters: A Division Of Labour	69
Preface	70
Rex, The Dish Maker	72
Chris, The Plate Maker	73
Doris, The Cup Handler	74
Terry, The Mould Runner	75
Hilda, The Fettler	76
Frank, The Manager	77
Barry, The Clay Carrier	78
Johnny, The Placer	79

Eric, The Plate Maker	80
Joe, The Director	81
Beryl, The Decorator	82
Alma, The Paintress	83
Edith, The Transferer	84
Dick, The Mould Maker	85
Vic, The Blunger	86
Dennis, The Slip Caster	87
John, The Student	88
Brian, The Union Man	89
Kath, The Office	90

Part I

On Biddulph Moor

I. What Justice In This Green Unpleasant Land?

Skint since the old man went, Bould had spied me
and Roy wog six eggs from his Barn Farm cote,
would teach us for good. Chased by a bobby –
I'd blubbed in court, slat down the bible, ran –
now I'm marked for life since everybody

read it up in the *Weekly Chronicle*
where I was aside the black lad of eight
who'd crept in a kitchen on Albert Street
and ate a whole iced second birthday cake.
Stammering he was clemmed, she didn't listen,
judged whipping would be best: some magistrate.
Blarting too, he'd leather clogs, no socks, shook
like the sparrer-legged Maeve who'd pinched five Weights
from Dirty Danny's shop. Spouting whether
girls who smoked should be thrashed or sent away,
Miss Fairey said the answer for her was
'fatherly guidance': no talk that Fridays

her dad thumped folk outside The Rose & Crown,
just the other week had thraped Sam Beech's dad
who'd been done for watering down the milk,
because they'd nothing mother reckoned, had
much less with the quarry shut, the locum
packing off their Stan to Barnardo's. Bad
enough shame stopped them coming to chapel

where conductor Jim Shuff had flopped it out
for cousin Rosemary in the vestry
after *Jesus Calls Us O'er The Tumult*.
She told but elders covered up his blame
for the Father's good name, left her at fault
as if her mini skirt had egged him on,
gave guilt for life, not three years like drunk Doc
Curry got for mowing Brown off his bike
outside the Hanging Gate, asking the boss
for a nip as sirens wailed, said, 'It might
have been worse, might have been me'. Not struck off,
still ginned, he examines the fatherless

where tourists trail for green not unpleasant
land, not muck-clogged ditches where poisonous
toads abandon broods into repellent
stinkhorned air and manky hands. What justice…?

II. And What Justice For Them

grown older with youthful shame
who with immense courage overcame
distressing libels on their dirtied names
or evil deeds while perpetrators became
snug survivors where fear damps truth and blame?

(after John Clare, *The Parish*)

The Egg Boy
I.

I was back pew sniggering at Walter Dishley's sermon text –
another law in my members, warring against the law of my mind.
And in my pants a law unto itself was taking shape seeded
by Linda Nixon's cross-legged stocking tops. Aroused
the black suit crowed and waved the bible at 'you thief back there,
laughing sinner scared to know this book. God will not forget
your sin. Repent or go in shame.' And at the turned faces, I fled
the bollockwash as if I had entered a temple where I had no right

to be, to make a mazy run of lefts and rights to Pleasureland,
swilling gallons of lousy beer, gorging on pies and chips,
food-mixing the brain on the Mad Mouse ride, gawping
at coloured light bulbs, turned on by flashing fruit machines
and high-heeled girls in Blackpool bars as jukeboxed Peggy Lee
asked *Is That All There Is?* And youth said yes, for now.

II.

Mown down, a morgue of neat swathes of the dead
grass, ladysmocks, buttercups laid out stiff
to dry waited to be pikel-tossed, raked
to rows, stooked for carting to the hayshed,

empty but for the stink of creosote
and muck midden; racked badging hooks, forks, scythes;
low rucks of last year's harvest. And Braddock
rigging up a swing from the thickest rope.

When he shoved real hard you could get so high
as to put your feet through the pitching hole,
see down the field across the Cheshire Plain
to Liverpool where big ships steamed, plumed sky

bubbling dreams like that Christmas annual:
the Elder Dempster Line's the *Aureol*
cargoed on her West African run, full
with mail, missionaries, guns, palm kernels.

Curving back, your head could split on an oak
beam: his three big lads, for dares, would miss it
by inches. Tall, I'd slow down well short. His
daughter Maeve, lozzucking on the hay, joked

I played too safe since court, scared to go too far,
showed me up in front of others, Ralph
Brown said she fancied me. Home one New Year,
we spoke, her loading kids into the car

in the coffin row built on the meadow;
the barn now parking for their caravan.
She'd wed a chapel bloke who sells you life
plans, buried her alive, bored work-widow

blurting that folk still missed me: had I been
abroad? I thought to brag that I'd risked it
all, sailed away to Freetown; played trombone
on Mardi Gras parades in New Orleans;

jammed with Kid Sheik near where sternwheelers plied.
But we've always been on a different
arc and, just in case she made me colour
up again, to close the circle, I lied.

Bobby Cole

They said I should have been Attorney General:
could read at two, play violin sonatas at four,
topped the eleven-plus for Wolstanton Grammar.
But there I fell in love with rugby, failed exams,
joined the Force. Doing night school law I dreamed
not of winning cases but scoring tries. And so I could
dive to tackle escaping lads, could make a game plan
to trap the village kiddie fiddlers. But that never made
my parents proud for they thought I was a genius. Never
did get round to telling them I didn't have the brains.

Roy

Half a dozen eggs! But for that sin
playground rats memorised my crime,
squeaked sneak thief, chanted their din
over and over like times tables
and *The Pied Piper of Hamelin*
I liked and then drew a picture of,
treated me like unloved vermin,

in shame drove me underground
to rip coal at Chatterley Whitfield
and to the lending library where I found
myself in poems and records, especially
love songs for my Decca player to pound
out: fell in love with Cilla Black, knew
them all. Tops? *The World I Wish For You.*

Bould

Chapel thoushaltnots sneaped us, blathered
shoulda give them thievin lads a second chance.
They bought others eggs an milk. Traited us
like sick beasts left to die in an owd shippon.
What'd they know safe wi god an wages from pits
an potbanks? What'd they know on scrattin
a livin from poor ground, forever bautered up
wi cack an nowt but werrit on money an bills?
Afe a dozen eggs is afe a dozen eggs. Am I raight?
I'd raither chuse straight than them pretendin things.
They deserved it. But weym ones traited as criminals.
As if weym's truth's a terrible offence. Well sod off.
Yowd hate this life. Them what asks what's up
I tell bugger off, tha's niver seyn a pig smile hast.

The Black Lad

Mother would stroke my hair, whisper
that I'm the sweet fruit of the seed
of a gentle, tall black soldier
billeted in the fustian mill,
tell that they'd danced to *In The Mood,*
went in the field then he never
came back from D-Day. She called me
Elmer like him to keep that love
and tenderness. She braved vile tongues.
And at school the other children
loved me, never saw my blackness
as I ran the fastest, laughing
and singing as I zoomed to win.
All so fine until that hunger
playing out that hot day before
Miss Fairey put me in that cage
for vile tongues to whip. Soured and scarred
I escaped to another place,
made a good life on the building,
wrote down some feelings, secret things
for him. Sometimes if I'm cornered,
or lonely, I wish that I'd searched
America, wish I could show
him my sayings, still stammer then.

Maeve

Sweet taste of Player's Weights! But not mucking out
the shippon right meant excuse for his strap for pinching
those fags from the village shop and showing him up. Till
a tractor overturned on him. To carry on mam took in washing
from the Faireys, traipsed it ironed over poached ground
which sucked its grip on every step, held the scrawny beasts
like posts. And over buried stiles that winter no one forgets
when blizzards piles against the hedges and daily filled
the snow-ploughs tracks. A gardener found her frozen stiff
by the Big House wall. Inside, dressed in silk she'd pressed,
they told Doc Foden she tried to do too much. Next day they
wrote me a note: a shirt was missing, to send it on. Years later,
I sold a field for building land for homes for locals. The Faireys
objected that bungalows would spoil their view of things. Well,
don't you think it's natural that I say, I'm glad they fucking well do.

Dirty Danny

Florrie my sister runs the shop since I did time. Still
all looks like normal village life; the front tin-plated
with *Craven "A"* and *Brasso*; the garage double doors
where lads thump shots at chalked-on goalposts
– in summer there's a wicket and they cricket topless
into dusk as spurts of dust from where the cork ball
pitches coat their glistening sweat. When the streetlight dies

I go down to do the till and locks, to breathe in paraffin;
cheese and bacon; coal tar soap; Vim; liquorice laces;
sherbet and pop. Back out, in a waft of cool night breeze
that makes me feel alive, above the crossbar, a poster
rustles *Vote Labour For Change.* Only four tacks pin it down,
stop the dream from breaking free and taking off. I dream of me

with damp boys on the deep pool's bank in the wooded
drumble hole where the stream has worn away the weakest rock.
When it's time to do the hens, I get out the Big Green Ticker
and on my way will cycle past to see if anyone is diving naked.

Miss Fairey

I have no qualifications beyond a training in magistrating
connections from a family background of importance
chair of charity committees and regular church attendance
and a belief in the sword of right and wrong, of wielding
it as a hater of law breakers and hater of making allowances
for the poor, crippled, widows, orphans. Compassion? I detest balance.
They think I am hard on their shortcomings but my sound judging
and rare mercy will make them clean and strong, give them a chance:
'Act well your part, there all honour lies.' said Pope. Me too: diligence,
duty. Yet at times as they pour before me, I wonder what is failing.

The Locum

I.

Thinner than me ghetto starving, whiter,
scalier than me forest deep after fleeing Warsaw,
his stick legs bony as those I saw in the camp
on bodies stacked like seasoned kindling,
I gagged on the bruised boy's pissed sheets.

They ate not much more than bread in milk
called pobs or bread in tea called soakies:
that's why I stethoscoped between his Belsen ribs
for the sputum ruckle. His window rattled
from a tanker sucking turds from their foul sty's
privy: for its stench they joked it the flower cart.
It shuddered the creamy hawthorn hedges
of that unsunned upland to which I went
to train to spear for free those such as him
with penicillin to make them better.

But what did better mean if in that hole,
if flayed meat, buckle wheals unhealed?
A Home could see him mend, bloom on beef tea.
And his mother would thank me for one less mouth.
So I reported, would not pass by or look away.

II.

Letters tell me he's doing well. For the practice
cast me out for high-souled resolution, sneered at
photos of purpled arms and paragraphs headed
Suppose no person living had any care for another
and *This boy is as much a part of things as Einstein.*
'It's not the way we do things. Diagnosis should show
no feelings,' they said. 'You foreigners are too emotional.
You'll be falling in love with one of them next' – as if
I should have been taught to avoid all gemmed blue eyes,
like those of the girl on the cattle train I never saw again
but look for, exiled back home where I tend sick children,
all as promising as young apples after blossom time.

Stan

The worker got it right when she said it
the best thing to have happened, the locum
sending me away to Barnardo's home,

that maybe I should think to thank him loads
because it had dead sure saved me from things
that dad was doing for years to our Sam.

Sam

He said I was special. So why let Danny?

I dream it was mother who told the bobby.

But *Best not talk* had scar-sealed *this wunna hurt*
till spannering off a wheel to mend some spokes
the wound sprang open, that croak welling up:
are tha comin' today? From Danny straddling
his bike – The Big Green Ticker. For the ride,
towed on his chicken feed laden cart
jangling up Stony Lane, grains flirting up, bouncing
to disused quarry hen pens, red pullets swarming
from creosote-stenched cotes to peck on broadcast
pellets of corn. Then his knee. The stubbly kiss.
The heat of it. *Dunna, dunna* to stop his jerking.
Tha munna tell only stopped when a bobby came,

the after buried till now's digging – for blame; guilt;
in assize court files; churning might-have-beens – like
touching or undressing in the light. And unlovedness:
was it because they thought it my fault? All this
with just you to tell that remembering didn't cause it,
it isn't misremembered, that there's no permanent repair
– even with whooping joy on learning of his death, that
just tarmacking over it like they did the lane years later.
I mean, how can I be happy while that smell of tar
lingers when hot sun bubbles the road on a summer day?

Beech

She went dry as a bone down there
and I belted her when she stopped my tap
so what's up with me naturally pleasuring
with the lad not ours though he doesn't know
we took him in when the coal cutter sliced his dad
And there might be a pro on market days at Leek

Others know but never bother and do far worse
Old Albie at his gate with his bag of toffees
when the kids come skipping out of school
Shuff in the vestry with his choir of little angels

Reckon they'd rather slag me for being the comer-in
who wouldn't believe the quarry was spent
who ignored that good advice about potatoes
and shake their heads as the Fordson ploughs
a crop of stones as I worry on how to pay
the pickers who search to fill half-empty sacks

Wish I'd kept on teaching English at Hanley High
and the prefect with an arse like a jelly on springs
rather than having to water down the milk
Reckon folk would rather shame me for that
rather shop me and get me done for the likes of that
than the other stuff   It's a subject on which
like poetry you see most people turn their backs

Jim Shuff

Under my baton I am the weaver-genius
of baritones and boy sopranos, organ-like
in their togetherness from my Black Dyke
banding bass days and grooming girls for the Orpheus

choir. They obey my every prick of the pure sung air
and with such status to do no wrong comes the power
to lie, to realise my fantasies, to not do guilt: the knower
of which child might give, how to get away with sin, taking care

no one else is there. And accusing my accusers, I meeken
them, hinting that I know of their own abuses behind
pig-eyed windows in smoky cottages, that I can find
them out of tune, deny them their precious music. Brazen

power I know and though their gossip makes me sick,
I have no conscience like my standing dick.

Doctor Curry

Everything they disgust at is true
in undertones as I pass, their dialect
disembowelling me in bars after I leave
but little do they know that this is paradise
compared to the three years in Strangeways
where they fucked me for my sins
before Doc Foden took me back, spoke up
for my doctoring skills and knowledge
gave me back my deserved status
and sent away the foreigner locum.

So I am free to stethoscope bare breasts again
to cup them for no good medical reason
other than to hear my obsessions sing –
some are rounded and feel just like silk
others are droopers like bottles of milk
– to see them bloom in slant sunlight
through half-shut surgery blinds
nipples huge and glinting as saucepan lids
me fondling while their men down shafts
phlegm coal dust blacker than my own filth.

I tell them I can find nothing wrong
will have to see them in a month
– I know my stuff you see –
sometimes see one in the back of the car
taking more care since I mowed down
Brown, the thud of his buckled face tossed
across the bonnet like a sycamore leaf
his mangled bike in the ditch
a twisted gut of tubing attacking me nightly.

I do it you see because I can
not because I failed psychiatry.
So waste no time probing for clues
about failed love or lust or some wound
that seeks oblivion in the bottle
or a secret buggered-baby story
locked in the poisons cabinet,
just allow me the arrogance
to say that they forgive me my sins
when they need me to make them better.

The Browns:
I. The Landlord

I gave him two bob and a Vimto
for the rabbit he'd brought. Thrilled,
he left: three girls in the chapel play.

Laying him in the snug, his face showed
not a trace of drink as I told the court.
And that they oughtn't to blame wet tarmac,
the blind bend or worn brake blocks
like that fancy Stafford lawyer tried.
Just khalied Curry. Thought I'd get
him done for good. Not three poxy years,
my say buried by the weight of suits
pressing to get their dirty verdict,
all smiles in the car park after.

The pub like a crypt for months, Brown
then crept back into our talk – what a good shot
he was, like Jane his eldest is. May
the youngest still seldom ever speaks
if seen; gardens, cleans for their mother.
Nell writes, has gone off the rails in Leek.

II. Nell

We blarted, knew something amiss
with him not turning up to see us
as blacked-up slave girls in
Golden Tales From Sunny Climes.

To carry on, Jane held fence posts,
mother swung the maul. May died inside,
sat days stock still like from a bomb blast,
went apieces, mute. I shouted at god
and his nuns who felt me up, kept me down
to one and one is, beat me to read what
the syllabus said. Said, 'Channel
your anger Nell, try sport.' Shove your
discus up your arse got me expelled

to find myself with stares at my holdall
on the market day bus; to live with books
in a sunny room; to be the arguing disliker
in gloomy bars; to dance and bawl out
All Of Me at the OkeyDokey Karaoke;

to risk all – putting foot to rock free-climbing
The Roaches' vertical crags and plunging

into that hidden language untaming my tongue
to write my grief in burning ink whenever dad calls.

Cousin Rosemary
I.

I was saved
by art and music

made a joyous life
through singing

avoided turning over the stone
for fear of the coiled worm

but when it did crawl out
into that old shaking hand

I stared over Bailey's Hill
into the daytime nothingness of space

where went the child in me
I would never see again like the years

where burned
those who denied me

where lived
the godless joy of the blues

where all of me
could be let go.

II.

To make a living each year I paint
for a show, watch the buyers' gallery tour
looking but seeing nothing
other than to decide on which frame colour
will match the shade of their lounge curtains,

escape to sing with The Delegates of Pleasure, moan
out *Give It To Me Slow.* Most nights end the same:
looking but seeing nothing
I pull, wake up and drive them away, blame
it on the blues for onenightstanding. Alone

I self-loathe for trusting no one
for not seeing all damage by their god is yet undone
in spite of my new-found faith that there is no god
where no one believes in god.

III.

He always got it right, my Uncle Jack:
excluded the meaningless. Look at his titles.

Old hay shed
Misty landscape
Cottages by a track
Two women and a child
Head and shed in snow
Lady's face on a hut by a tree
Telegraph pole, ladders, stone wall
Outbuildings, tree and dark figure
Figure with barn beyond
Man, woman and tree
Figures in a dark lane
House with lean-to
Cow and shed
Twilight

All black, white and grey the critics said.
But when he showed me how he painted,
his eyes shone like only a poor child's can,
shone black with happiness showing me
the buried vibrancy, how to make it
shine through when he wanted it to:
terracotta. And his favourite, old gold.

IV.

Framed by the opening of a derelict barn,
no company but for creaking rafters,

I have worked all day, my prepared canvas
now a picture of distant bottle kilns and slagheaps,

a rock-jagged skyline towards the misted Troughstones,
drystone walls, hawthorn hedges, tiny pastures, a spring

which will stream to become the River Trent,
scythemen arcing their way up Braddock's meadow,

huddled cottage clusters half-hidden on shadowed slopes
as scudding Potteries smoke plumes blacken the palette.

I have painted the surface, what you can see anyway
and the what goes on: look at the drawn faces.

I start to clean the brushes. A light goes on
in an upstairs room. My dab of orange brings it to life

as too inside where memories have flared
and someone has risen and started to write.

Glossary

p 9
wog – to steal
blub – to cry
slat – throw down
aside – next to
clemmed – hungry
blart – to cry
sparrer-legged – skinny
spout – talk a lot
thrape – to thrash
egg-on – encourage
manky – filthy

p 12
pikel – pitchfork
badging hook – hand scythe
lozzucking – idle, lounging or laying around

p 15
sneaped – snubbed
traited – treated
shippon – cowshed
scrattin – scraping
bautered – splashed with mud or cowshit
cack – excrement
werrit – worry

p 17
traipsed – trudged wearily
poached – trampled, muddy from overgrazing

p 18
drumble hole – wooded valley between fields

p 27
khalied – drunk

p 28
maul – heavy sledgehammer to drive in stakes, posts
apieces – broke up

Part II

Hereabouts and Thereabouts

A Thank You To Biddulph Library

Kept down to one and one is two led to woodwork
and Sunday school teachers forcing prayed thanks
to im above for his education gifts that got you only fit
to cut coal at Black Bull pit or saggar pots for bottle kilns
till mother took and joined me to my spiritual saviour

on the way to where on the Saturday morning bus
chapel thoushaltnots sniggered and thought me queer
head in a novel alone with a bag of heathen books
them unknowing the thrill of that lending card
as passport to explore another world to satisfy
a thirst for knowledge born of untrue sermons
and to journey reborn in that reading room womb
where the air was warm and sweet with words

And I came out knowing of science and wars
speaking of lunar mountains and craters
rainforests and deserts and African savannahs
of how to bat like Bradman bowl like Tyson
rich in football wisdom from Stanley Matthews
or spouting about Nietzsche and his not joy
but joylessness being the mother of debauchery
or philosophising on the littleness of man
and greatness in Paul Robeson and Rosa Parks
learning from Shakespeare what this drama means
or finding where I stand in the scheme of things
in Orwell's politics of them and us then for Milligan
to blunt it with nonsense and crease me up
and discovering fiction where a hero taught me
to take care criticising those without my advantages
and it all right to write *horseness is the whatness
of allhorse* and of arcs in urinating competitions
and that there no guilt in touching a back to a quiver
tucking in the label of a smokeblue summer dress
and from borrowed records found the hymns of soul
with love songs for my Dansette to pound out
learning by heart ones like Etta James's *At Last* ...

and... the spell was cast for with these insights
that search for me began and above all from learning
by heart from the vision of poets moulding language
to make sense of it all to *construct at last a human justice*

And so thanks to the gifts of that place I am democratized

The Half-A-Crown

The news delivers the dead like cricket scores, deadpan.
And with no god jumping off a cloud to help or guess
a future, today I crave past truths to ease the dread, am
coop-flown to The Hanging Gate, newsing and joshing
on whatever happened to Pamela Machin when Frank
pronounces: *all memories grow into childhood.* And
right then unbottled this pouring out of a gone world

how Hezekiah Bailey, who wouldn't let a tractor
on his land, had found a fortnight of weather when
he tapped a rising glass and the wireless gave no rain
to begin his scything and till the mowing done, slept
under a hedge bedded in hessian hen corn sacks,
dropping off to nightjars whirring in the wood, of

how he fed from linen bundles and jugs of nettle beer
his children brought then when his sharpening whetstone
clank had frit the larks and peewits, marked their nests
with hawthorn sticks to save them from his blade, of

how he would send the village folk a call for help
with the scorching hay after his wife had lit an apronful
to show it ready. And we came, shoving two oak poles
called stangs under each hubbled ruck, carted them
sedan chair-like to the barn where he'd pikel the piles up
through the pitching hole till dusk then, face to face, gave
me and Frank and Pamela his thanks – and half-a-crown,

his fairness and the coins cupped gently like new-found eggs,
walked slowly home to share – now that needed fragment
of sense to share before being curfewed back to the pen
and *here we are and what the hell are we going to do about it.*

Laughter Lines for Hanley High

The history class cracked up when I joked
that Mr Maddock had told us a mere Jaffa ruled
as a warlord rather than the Emir of Jaffa. So
criminal guilty of causing grievous laughter, I am
in a cabbage-stenched detention hall,
my fountain pen reams out futility,
no boredom remission but for the BOLLOCKS
compass-carved in capitals by a disused inkwell,
my caned, bruise-fattened arse throbbing clenched
as hunched anger scribbles a thousand lines:
I must not act daft.

Across the aisle, for yapping in English Language
Norman Jones must now churn out five hundred
Empty vessels make most noise
next to Donald Tink who left French homework
on the bus so is now imprisoned for a thousand
When a man is idle, what doth
it most of all behove him to do?

Outside, council houses and smoke-sheened hills play
sight-screen for good boys cricketting in fading light,
overs spinning towards a finish long before Tink,
his tea gone cold, his mother worried sick,
his father waiting ready with the strap.

Done, I jab my foolscap script into Shellshock Sid
still with shakes from the Somme. Pages trembling,
he stammers some of it is rushed, illegible, and
makes no sense. None of it I think before he blurts,
'G-go b-boy. And l-let that b-be a l-lesson to you.'
Still sore, I am not sorry for his cruel consonants
but do not snigger like resting Tink who rubs away
wrist cramp gazing out to the mist-wisped pitch.

Only he is left as I stump down empty corridors
wafted through with the scent of outfield mowing
to an evening that unfurls in a bloom of words.
After the essay on *How Green Was My Valley,*
unfettered, I twizzle through humming and crackle
from the wireless dial, searching for the Light
and Third Programmes: plays, talks, jokes, songs,
poetry – language for pleasure not punishment. And
The Goons to make nonsense of it all, to crease me up.

Coming Home For The Funeral

The plastic valve in your heart packed up. Would I be a bearer?
Mother's voice shaky to the office from the village phone,
coins running out to the silence of why you. And what to wear
– white shirt crisp from British Home Stores cellophane
to show respect; whether to iron half-decent trousers
after sponging off lime pickle pips and stag-do stains;
buffing up my only proper shoes to get your father's
nod; sports jacket to Sketchley's for their special offer clean.
Then the smarten up trim and shave at the station barber's;
black knot tightened in the toilet mirror before the train

pulled in to what remains: no pit for work, *The Goose* gone
for match day pints – but everywhere, you. So I wish you knew
my fury at the minister's eulogy: it could have been for anyone.
Shouldering you out, I was glad I'd made the effort – to hold you.

What Might Have Been

Someone will sidle up at a corporate do
and say, *Didn't I see you in The Simbolics,*
on bass, at The Place in Stoke, about '62?
And I'm back; pulling groupies in local clubs;
on a college tour, opening for The Who;
trashing a hotel room with Moon. Still have
demo tapes that nearly got a record deal after two
auditions for Mickie Most. But when Sim died,
ploughing into a milk float in his brand new
Mini after a 100 Club all-nighter, so did we.
Cocking-up on what to call ourselves after too
much booze, hecklers would chant *The Bolics*
are a load of you know what and we grew
to be The Knackered Three more like, reduced
to churning out weary standards and Lulu
and the Luvvers covers at weddings and functions.
But entertaining gets in the blood and few
can give it up. These days we've injected
comedy into what we do, go out as (this is true)
Jock Strapp and his Two Swingers. The thing is,
we're on the up again, have invested in blue
satin stage suits and new equipment. Good news is
it's paying off: next year we provide support to
Jane McDonald on a Caribbean cruise. It keeps
the tax man happy: but if only he knew
what might have been. Macca used to mail me.

In The 1930s: I. Them and Us and The Holditch Colliery Disaster

At her first party this season at which debutantes were presented and where funds were to be raised to support refugees from the Spanish Civil War, the Duchess of Biddulph, who cut short a holiday in Scotland in order to be present at the ball, received the Duchess of Horton with Mrs Arnold Wincey, on whom, as Viscountess Southsea had not been well, fell the responsibility of arranging most of the details connected with the ball. The previous year Mrs Wincey had organised a ball to raise money to buy shoes for the Jarrow unemployment marchers on their arrival in London. Everyone was unanimous in praise of her efforts, charm and sweetness again this year. The Countess of Tunstall, who wore a bright green chiffon dress, seemed especially interested in a donated small Peke puppy, which she duly handed over to a lucky winner in the course of the evening's fundraising prizegiving. Lady Gratton, in black, with earrings and bracelets of black jet, was one of the smartest women in the ballroom. She likes original clothes and is not afraid to wear them. Mrs Charles Cockin would look lovely in sackcloth, but she wore a really beautiful dress of black lace over a pink foundation. She and her husband had come on from the Curzon Cinema, where 'Things Are Looking Up' and 'Forever England' had been given as a first-night double-bill premiere performance in aid of Mrs. Cuthbert Swain's Feathers Clubs for poor children, a companion venture to her Feathers Clubs for distressed older people. This was one of the smartest of several first showings of films last week including 'Off The Dole' featuring Mr. George Formby. The German Ambassador Mr. Joachim von Ribbentrop was welcomed. Other guests at the ball included Coronation visitors from overseas, some wearing native dresses, like those from the Solomon Islands, Australia, North Africa, Trinidad and other colonies. The visit of Mrs. Baldwin, the Prime Minister's wife, was necessarily brief. She had come from a meeting at the Ladies' Carlton Club and was due in Eaton Square to fulfil another fundraising engagement for the wives of the thirty miners who died in the Holditch Colliery explosion in Staffordshire. Many Conservative M.P.s came in during the evening. Early arrivals left to return to the House of Commons to vote on the Vote of Censure, and returned again, including Mr. Churchill, to celebrate the Government's defeat of the censure motion against the Government's support for the Spanish fascists in acquiescing to their blockade against our ships in the Bay of Biscay preventing their entry into the port of Bilbao. They enjoyed an evening which, starting with a reception and music from the band of Sir Ken "Snakehips" Johnson at half-past nine, very soon developed into a most enjoyable dance. The wife of the Earl of Malvern and her party left early to fulfil an engagement the following morning when she was due to greet the disembarkation at Southampton docks of 4,000 Basque child refugees of the Spanish conflict and dispense warm broth, donated by the Charity for the Deserving Poor, to all those deemed to be in need.

II. A Short History Of The Great Depression

REV. E. DAVID EDWARDS.

EPWORTH HOUSE,
BIDDULPH,
STAFFS.

August.10.1936.

Dear Sir,
      The bearer, Mr. Wilson Lancaster is anxious to secure some form of employment. I can confidently recommend him to any person willing to give him a chance. He will prove himself worthy of the confidence of any employer. He is trustworthy and willing, thoroughly conscientious. His health is not robust having only recently recovered from a long illness. His immediate concern is some form of occupation (not wages). I have seen some of his work, and have no hesitation in declaring him to be a good workman. He deserves every encouragement.

yours truly,

E. David Edwards

TELEPHONE Nos 284 285
TELEGRAPHIC ADDRESS
"CONLOWE" CONGLETON

ALL COMMUNICATIONS TO BE ADDRESSED TO
BROWN STREET MILLS

DIRECTORS:-
W A LOWE C H BROTHERTON
T F TATTERSALL E V MONK

FACTORIES:-
BROWN STREET MILLS, CONGLETON
DANE BRIDGE MILL, CONGLETON
DANE MILL, CONGLETON
TOWN MILL, SANDBACH

Conlowe Ltd.

MANUFACTURERS OF KNITTED GOODS
FROM RAYON, WOOL AND COTTON
LADIES' AND CHILDRENS' UNDERWEAR,
SLUMBERWEAR AND OUTERWEAR
ALSO MENS' UNDERWEAR AND SPORTSWEAR

BROWN STREET MILLS

CONGLETON.

IN YOUR REPLY PLEASE REFER TO
ACCOUNTANTS DEPT.

August 12th, 1936.

Mr W. Lancaster,
Biddulph Moor.

Dear Mr Lancaster,

    I thank you for your letter dated August 11th, but much regret that, at the present time, we do not seem to have any suitable vacancy which we can offer you. I am, therefore, returning herewith the testimonial which you sent on to me, but I am having a further look round and, if anything turns up, I shall be only too pleased to let you know.

    Yours sincerely,

CONLOWE LTD.

FP/PW.

A Wesleyan Sunday School Outing

Candy floss energy spent and sea air knackered
try-sleep children woke as on the bus front rows,
fired up by soapbox preachers on the beach that dusk,
a choir of clapping teachers struck up a rousing
Jesu lover of my soul let me to thy bosom fly
joined by harmonies from half-cut elders, red-faced
from sinful gins in the Lifeboat Inn, all so tranced
no one saw through fag smoke to back seat goings-on
where Robert Shufflebottom unbuttoned a blouse
as Blackpool prom got turned on and illuminated.

At Biddulph Wakes

Savage's Famous Thundering Gallopers:
a safe and gentle ride they said. But you
grip the twisted, golden, barley-sugar pole,
eyes tight-shut to the huge, bared teeth
and panic-painted, cocked left eye
of the bucking horse's head. Others whoop,
laugh – at you, you think. And you wonder
why you cannot share the fun.
                                        Down there,
among the pointing faces, only your father,
the fixed point on every circuit, understands.
He will lift you down, talk you through
the early years, say everything will be
all right, his kid-gloved hand easing you
through the crowd to win a goldfish in a bowl.
Just for you. Just the once.

Sussed: Cobridge 1974
...light falls equally on black and white (W. H. Auden)

I shelled equality's skin-thin husk that summer dusk
shed the upbrought moral of try to see the good in all

walking to work a late shift   feeling good with the lift
from an all-OK swoon of a lovemaking afternoon
craning to kiss her neck as she slept like lain porcelain
pub lager and lime as Pawson's horn caressed *Sweet Adeline*
before a mown park grass scent stroll   tall tree-shadows bent
as fire-rose melted to violet painting the edge of night
muted as my jazz and Marley-soothed ears

                                        till I ran in fear
from wailing sirens   cars spewing truncheons
that beat and boots that kicked with looks
through visors all hate   a hate hard to exaggerate
one keeping me down   pinned to the ground
foot on my cock and trampling dreadlocks
asked if rastafairies live in the bottom of my garden
as an arm-gash bled to decorate handcuffs that led
to a cell for a three days stay   boss unknowing why I'm away
in July 1974 under Section 4 of The Vagrancy Act 1824
for nothing done wrong except my lips belong
to those of my race they said photofitted the 'cullud' face
suspected of robbing an office

                         so sussed   as we say   racist
injustice burned with time and freedom lost for no crime
big busted lips silent in a vow to wage war on the unfair law
both bad legislation and uniforms disgracing their station

unlocked   not free   they forced a signed lie of mistaken identity
no apology   a lie buttered smooth as doctored television news
that year of riots against wrongs people could take no longer

at the taxi   Rosie gently eased me in   and eyes spat at her skin
called her slag as if to be with me an arrestable offence to log

but home   love salved anger   and bruises with tincture of arnica
and the dabbing late sun   which glinted our downy arms as one

Still Cutting It

Waiting for the curtain to rise
before the compere's *Hands together, let's hear it for…*
at Cobridge British Legion, or the weekly job at
La Verda Stelo on Smallthorne's Esperanto Way,
Spock would work the alto keys to a nervous rattle,
like one of his marionette's dancing wooden bones,
with fingers chisel-scarred, cut-healed from his other love:
you need just the same caress and feel he'd say. That touch.

Gig-years on, it finally fell
on lungs burned-out by smoke from Pirate Shag tobacco.
He'd been eaten away to starving-thin, whittled
down fine as one of his owl-headed holly walking sticks.
We cleared his place in half an hour: bed, two easy chairs,
pine table, hand-made chest of drawers, tools, Selmer sax,
the old Dansette and a box of jazz, mostly Parker,
Rimington, Barnes and Cap'n Handy, the ones he learned from
and could never part with, not for any money. And
in the foodless fridge to stop the green wood drying out,
labelled blocks of basswood, ash, butternut, apple, pear:
a half-carved bowl and serving spoon in cherry and plum

for his Newcastle shop, window
for his *art, if you like*, to call to others. Out back,
him gouging grooves, ideas in wood, we'd play new tracks.
Now when I play the crackly 78 I kept
of Konitz blowing *Skylark,* it's him I hear soaring
from that meadow in a mist. Or see, after storms in
Hanley Park, cutting broken boughs for that treasure hoard.

Is There Anything You Would Like To Ask Us?

See you've moved about a lot. Experienced but unreliable
seemed to be the tone of buttoned-up waistcoats.
*We need someone to see this project through. Stability.
Three years minimum.* Single at forty came next, gay or
weird pulsing from foreheads. *Well-qualified from your
CV; master's, doctorate.* Over-qualified, perpetual student
neat in capitals on company logoed notepads I imagined.
Please tell us why you applied. To watch sweat stains grow
green in bri-nyloned armpits a demon said. *Do you
feel computer literacy essential..?*

                      I drifted to the tipping point, it
being where the ear stops to let in clicking heels of girls by the
sea in blowy summer dresses or a child on bass trombone or
De De and Billie Pierce singing *All Of Me.* What puts arse to
see-saw just past where futility says sod this, go find yourself
freed from this courtroom reliance on judgment by others, put
feet on rock…What?   .

                    Computers? Sorry, run through that again. *EYE
TEE?* No. Brain, hand, pen, paper, me. *Not even use a Dictaphone?*
Me? No, just a finger like everyone I know. *Is there..?* No. A train
leaves for Stoke in half an hour. So thank you all, I really have to go.

The Home Game
(for Alan Lobos)

Once we had a country and we thought it fair.
Look in the atlas and you'll find it there;
We can never go there now, my dear...
          (from Song by W.H. Auden)

How easily I talk of torture friends say,
matter of fact about burn scars. Yet
how they hurt on team photos. Lines too
around my eyes, worn dark as folds
in old family letters, read and read, even
painful ones just with news of funerals
and telling of ever less hope; the dust
of the rubble will not settle; we have
not begun to build the new way; for
escaping, it's still not safe for you; Lydia
raped by soldiers needs a wheelchair.

So they came, children growing to hate
to hear Jara's songs, to dance cueca,
moaning in perfect English. It choked
like the piss-bucket stench in solitary
in that cell under the National Stadium:
a tiny window let you watch guards
footballing on the bright green pitch,
to play there my homeland dream.

Hard going back when a regime falls
I read. But did: into a gone past of dead
ideals, comrades changed, icy voices
saying I'd had an easy exile, no hero
like the disappeared, made me know
I wasn't the same, my dream a myth
lifeless as scorched turf that summer.

The flight back ended a stolen time. Back
to blown leaves swirling with curses
in mother tongue babble at park referees
and foreign mud sucking on my studs
for yet another season, still in attack
for Los Chilenos, reigning champions,
Division V, Potteries Sunday League.
And settled on the touch-line, that girl,
cheering papa till every final whistle,
waiting to be pushed to where is home.

Channel-Hopping With The Barman

He flicked from luxury cruises to political pundits
to rolling news of warsick famine-fleeing nomads
bailing noosing waves from blow up boats, mute
till he told the screen and us happy-hour listeners
the exile-crowded sea is nothing new, how it did
for him and his brother too in paying a heavy price
to map another life, forced to leave the Wexford farm
so their folks didn't have to sell, the year crops failed,
how on the Rosslare ferry laden with other workless
Leinster men and women they'd lined the bar, all talk
of what they'd become to make their mothers proud
and rich with oceans of money in the post, make them
heroes like rugby stars once back in their fabulous land.

Now he serves their likes with rakes of stout
as stiff they come at six from dented vans
after lifting spuds and leeks in freezing fields
or soaked from labouring on building sites. And
he'd been that side; spouting of last night's craic
at work; of work in the pub; which gangers paid
more dosh an hour; where to get a cheaper bed;
pinning all hopes on the tails of donkey dreams

– a long shot coming in; the real one coming along;
the going home for good – hurdles flattened by pints
into a race to see how far memories could be ridden
soundtracked by exile's vicious freedom to roar rebel
songs or replay *The Wild Rover* over and over till closing
and drinking up with incanted promises to dying fathers;
how it could be worse; yearnings for what they'd lost,
then all torture soothed with a rosary of towns and villages
where everyone knew them, somebody loved them
and of the miracle of a man who sat on top of a pole
for days at annual fairs and of a woman who would fart
a chorus of *Danny Boy* for a sixpence, her stenched tent
flapping with laughter. He'd reel off their tales and places
as if from his own uncut umbilical cord – of Tubbercurry,
Killorglin, Mullingar, Mullagh, Ratoath – his cracked voice

showing he shared what they felt. And tonight, with anger
jabbing off the remote, saying nothing changes, cursing
brainless shame-shod politicians unbothered by who might
be hauled up fish-eye glazed in tomorrow's tidemark catch.

The Island Surveyor

Distant all week drawing up field notes,
she cracked at Friday's lunchtime glass, how

the chance to chart her roots turned
sour near Kilkenneth's marram-grassed dunes.
By a ruined kirk and some run-down
crofts, a boy and girl had watched her take
readings, holding hands followed close past
grazing cattle to the islet. West,
the Atlantic fetch to that bastard
Canada to where his broken folks
were herded, the factor's stick, no work
mapping their future, her dad given
to Glasgow aunts who took him to grieve
them off: how his arm ached *till their waves
grew tiny, snuffed out by funnel smoke*
he'd say when they got the photos out.
And after; their deaths by telegram.

Folding her theodolite, she'd shooed
off the wains, plotted roofless remains
in ripe cornfields – those evicted lives
and those children's chances haunting her
anger since.

      She raged – the politics
of how it was, how it ought to be –
then filled up, had to get back, slowly
zig-zagging through the lounge, as if great
foundation stones were chained to her feet.

Sex Education at Boots

So it's the old hydraulics then? said the pharmacist
blowing my anonymity to prescription queuers
reducing an intended whisper to a croak:

This Viagra: does it work?
Every time, sir. Never fails.
I believe you can get it over the counter?
Only if I take two, sir. He smiled

and to a choir of titterers and a woman mumbling
it disgusting in a man my age, I coloured up,
fled ashamed as if escaping again from youth club
laughter when they twigged that I knew nothing
of pulling or going all the way or muff diving
or getting slacked off or trying it on or full sex or
a good feel in the field with experienced Phoebe –
who wouldn't let me near her with a cattle-prod. Me,

still trapped, stumbling through their maze of codes,
zig-zagging to another exit past Fetherlites and lubes
racked like those phobias I dream of curing. I mean,
what is 'full sex'? Will I get stroking of hair and hands
and a back that quivers at my touch as I tuck in the label
of a blue summer dress like novels imagine? And
a cupped tummy rising and falling faster and faster
with a weight pressing down till it must explode?
Will there be a window spilling sun on a downy neck?
Will I not feel shame at undressing in that light?

Baldwin's Iron and Steelworks, Swindon

Double digging, each spring her spade will clank on metal:
last year a twisted bar, now some rusted plate as if the mill
rolls on, pushing up artefacts to exhibit its past. And her past

too – snug in *The Green Man,* once works-owned to flog a pint
to thirsty rollers and catchers between heat runs, her dad still
drinks to nationalisation, spark-blasts fireworking 'British Steel'
in a smoke-stenched sky that day; a redundant husband promised
hope but on a daily towpath mope where narrowboat coalers plied
the cut to fuel his days and grass whish and birdsong replace the din;
the groan of sheet and girder walls felled and flattened in demolition,
cleared for her son to labour on the new estate; the terrace to semi flit
and soot-free washing in *Swin Forge Way,* named so as not to forget.

Like at each back end, forking seams of spuds and, as if it hadn't died,
a crop of clinker and slag from a furnace never fully doused.

The Search

It was just like grieving
until the kids had phoned
to say they'd not been near
the bomb. To try to make
sense of the why of it,
I ran to my river
thinking place. From the bank,

cruise boats tannoying that
from my viewpoint Turner
moved the church to compose
a better painting and
skinny-dipping child-whoops
returned the world to sane
and couldn't get any worse

till night's siren-spooked geese
walloped their wings to lift
over reed shafts, fizzed low
upstream, an arrowhead
firing its warning honks
of undertows, too late,
for fraught head-torched parents
who swept the dark calling

a name. Blue-grey first light
shaped its answer – curled up
like a question mark
bedded in low tide mud.

Anniversary

Someone snapped their childhood,
clogged, hand-in-hand,
captured innocence,
the fun of the mean Tunstall alleys,
before the background smog
rolled down, wrapped them together,
trapped them in the smells
of lecked summer dust, their own kind,
marriage – which seemed escape
then a cage. Though Australia's
blanket of blue had tempted. Too far,
they'd moved in without ever moving out
then watched the bonded bricks torn down
and them and the children, friends, split up
allocated out to Chell or Weston Coyney.

Hand-cuffed by birth, births
Port Vale scarves, unchanging years,
kept down to *one and one is...*
can't you read what this says?...
get yourself a job at Price's Teapots
or down the pit at Whitfield,
see them shake it off for this
as the video rolls at the special do
at Chell Heath British Legion. See them
duet on *You're The One I Care For*
though she has always made the best of it
and he once said it never brilliant.
See them wear their smiles tonight
like wedding dresses dancing in the street,
tomorrow tight like stocking masks.
See them worn, stretched out.
What presses from their dreams?
See them without. Or making love again
on Troughstones. Or sleeping back-to-back.

The Wedding Speech

It began with not the usual phone call.
You know, another loan for the rent deposit on a flat,
another box of climbing gear and skis to store,
another ask to find that degree certificate…

No, this time just help to fix a 'sort of chandelier.'
'It's the weight,' he said. 'And it's for Anna's room.'
A bit above and beyond your landlady's call I thought.
But when I saw the light – boulder-heavy as the moon,

rat's maze wiring diagram – I understood, knew this must be
for someone special. I said, 'We'll need to find the joist,
use three-inch screws.' 'Not my taste,' he muttered,
his fingers crimping to hold it straight

while I tightened the rose, his footholds smeared firm
on the wobbly steps, like on the seaside cliffs
we could not keep him away from as a child. From
wild crags and flexible friends to Anna's DIY 'v. diff.'!

But seeing the care when he fiddled so gently
to get the thousand glass droppers dangling just right,
it felt like I was watching an act of love.
Switching on, admiring our handiwork, sorry, but that great

smile of his beamed as if a new route bagged, topped out.
Driving back, I got that funny floaty feeling
you have when you know someone might be right. Remember?
And later when he phoned to say Anna says thanks for helping

and that she thinks that it looks just great,
his voice held that lightness, always for us a sign
in him of happiness, a happiness that we all want, wish
for them now. And for a long and peaceful time.

Case Notes
(for Dr Oscar Lancaster, wishing him less night shifts)

He said Mr Cahill could recall The Troubles, playing
trombone in Big Mick's Showband back in Sligo
– but not that his wife is dead or his children's names.
The capacity test had scored him delirious a day ago.
Today he asked where his house is as he was guided
back to bed, next to Mr Jones who knows

he's ninety-two and asks why he's there,
why he's made to wear a mask. He enthuses
about being a fisherman in Antigua and seeing
West Indies beat England in 1950, knows who
scored what – but not his children's names. His test
score is delirious, like Mr Cahill – but less confused.

In the afternoon, a nurse had to stop Mr Cahill
from trying to dress Mr Jones to take him to town.
As she'd undressed Mr Jones, Mr Cahill had said
that Mr Jones is his wife. Replacing his gown
she told him Mr Jones is not his wife. He said,
'I thought she was looking rather brown.'

Going home, Oscar stopped at their curtained bay.
Like dumbed visiting relatives, word-spent,
they sat face to face holding and stroking
each other's hands, both smiling, lover-silent
in that floaty feeling of discovery. Looking
all there, as they say. But, who knows, how different.

From Kumasi to Kidsgrove
or The Missionary Position In That Wind Of Change

1955

Dear Father, At the call of God, at last the Gold Coast!
Full of joy, I could not sleep last night for the great heat
and the urge to begin my chosen task of leading the eager
multitudes into the full light and knowledge of Christ. I rejoice
to have this glorious opportunity and privilege. Not since
He called me to train at Wesley College have I felt such joy.
So far away from doing accounts at the shirt mill and traipsing
the moor to preach to nine in freezing chapels to this oven
of a room and still palm trees not hawthorn and sycamores
at my window. This stillness. No more that sickness from the liner
rolling. How many fellow Methodists would give their eyeteeth
for this chance to teach the Word in place of idols and ignorance?
Fellow missionaries say ignorance is the biggest barrier – for me
it's this airmail page confining my excitement. Pray for me.

•••

Today I wrestled for three hours with five black men
wanting salvation but unable to make the great surrender
who faced me with a barrage of questions on sex which
shows that the Holy Spirit is convicting them of sin. Men
are everywhere seeking God. If only they can be brought
to the point of surrender! Please pray for me, that God may
use me. My time is short. Soon they will leave the mission
for good. They must be saved within the month. Please gather
a group to pray every day for conviction and conversion. Your
prayers mean so much: God uses them mightily as a source
to channel His power. Pray! Pray! Pray and the blessing will
break. The weather is getting cooler now: the dry season
Harmattan has begun and the north wind lays Saharan dust
through every crevice. Now I really must pray then get to bed.

•••

1956

Sorry am late – things on my mind, now discharged. Not least
to reconsider my work here after battering away with the natives,
twelve months with precious little visible result. It's led me through
Him to a new approach after a spiritual spring cleaning. Now I see
a general seeking through My Absolute Dedication and God
has opened many doors – Christ must be taken inside with wonderful

opportunities to commend The Saviour: local wireless Christmas talks
and Mampong Boys' Camp, occasions when all kinds of future leaders
can be converted. Pray for them and me that the right words are spoken
that men may be saved like last Sunday. Planned at a mission service,
my sermon was on *If thirst be not raised etc.* It coincided with a
memorial service for a murdered village woman. I believe some good
resulted: it made me feel spiritually fully alive. Please ask mother to send my
old tobacco tins. Hope you're impressed I've learned to type. Every blessing.

...

Hope you get this. Posted up country to a large village mission
for a month before Christmas. The atmosphere was somewhat
strained for a time due to an unfortunate rumour that spread rapidly
round the District to the effect that Europeans were kidnapping
and cooking African children for their Christmas dinner. The story
started with the death of an African child in a nearby Christian-run
hospital and the European nurse having a hand in packing the body
off to Accra for post-mortem. How you can see that God is needed.
It's wild country compared to Kumasi. But apart from inevitable
spearings and murders after beer-drinking parties, it's law-abiding
with tribal discipline still effective. But does my preaching get through
or matter? Should I write? As my Thomas Adams says; 'Our books may
come to be seen, where ourselves shall never be heard. These may preach
when the other cannot, and (which is more) when he is not.' I wonder.

...

Took Good Friday services in college and feasted after. But missed
pickled onions and the sausage rolls and Stoke oatcakes we'd get
at the chapel tea. And Home & Colonial ham! Easter Monday went with
friends to the Ashanti Gold Mine: there is a lovely swimming pool
for the staff which other Europeans are allowed to use. Good fun but
for sullen Ashanti attendants and a demonstration outside
with placards for independence. No trouble though with the mine's
own armed security guards on hand. Over waakye (beans and rice)
– but no wine for us Methodists! – the mine manager spoke
of growing unease over independence with local riots after vans
blaring the Convention People's Party message through megaphones
had toured the villages. When I got back, prayed long and hard
that the Word of God would prevail and overcome any turmoil.
My back got terribly burnt at the pool but feels much better now.

...

Times are changing. You may soon hear of riots in Kumasi.
The CPP government is trying to pass an anti-chieftaincy bill
which is very unpopular in Ashanti. If it is passed there may be
civil disorder. There is no need to worry about us Europeans
as long as we keep our noses out of it. True the rebels don't like us
and our rule but this is a black man versus black man palaver
and I don't think the English stock has ever stood so high
after all we have done for them in developing the country.
There is a very genuine affection for the white man here.
There is so much corruption among the native politicians
and professions that the whites are regarded as very necessary
in guarding against the decay of public life and moral standards.
Must close now but please pray for us whom appointed by God
to minister Salvation to such a needy people in unsettling times.

...

1957

At the beginning of last month we had all the excitement
of independence: quite a historic occasion with special services
and many public functions – and two days holiday! But I am
convalescing from a war with some students. They want to return
to the old tribal ways. Some taunt me by wearing fetich charms
to class and, laughing, chant as if to call up the supposed magical
powers. They left a curse on me. I pray for them. And other things
decline. As more and more Africans take over senior positions
in the country there is a corresponding increase in inefficiency. At
independence the railways managed to produce a train which did
a circular tour from Accra to Takoradi via Kumasi in something
like decent time: after a fortnight it had to be taken off service.
Perhaps we should have trained them better. The electricity
fails on average once a night. Must finish before it makes me end.

...

Things in independent Ghana are not too happy at the moment.
There seems to be a general depression among the Europeans here.
And missionary work is hard. Some converts have now become
backsliders who have forsaken God for the new politics. One
spat at me and said that all who preached God and believed in God
were destroying the future of Ghana and wasting their own lives.
But my faith holds and physically I have never felt better in my life.
I recommend the life here to anyone. Provided one takes the routine
precautions there is no reason why one should not be healthier
than in England, certainly we're not pestered with colds and flu
though the recent weather has been very trying for all, afternoon

temperatures being 90 degrees in the shade. But the past few days
have seen showers so we can hope the rainy season is approaching.
We have a glut of lettuces. We eat them *twice* a day. Pray for us.

...

Thanks for the new shirt and news of cousin Joyce's baby. Tell
mother not to worry about my safety though the Prime Minister
Dr Kwame Nkrumah shows disturbing traits which remind one
of the familiar pattern of dictators. He has pinched the Governor's
castle to live in himself and decided to replace the impartial civil
service Chief Regional Officers (sort of Area Governors) by
nominees of his own party. And in a speech the other day he talked
of prosecution (sorry, persecution) of the Jehovah's Witnesses
because they refuse to vote in elections and hinted at the same time
of possible action against other religious bodies which might annoy
him. I haven't much time for the Jehovah's myself but I don't like
any kind of persecution. As congregations fall, I talk with colleagues
about whether our work here has been in vain. My mission for God
feels unwanted. I must confess to thoughts of returning home.

...

1958

Thanks for the birthday card. It got here eventually – a week late.
The postal service once reliable when run by us is getting worse
like the railways I told you about some time ago. And I am feeling
very low – the congregations at chapel and bible classes continue
to fall. And some classes have become unteachable. Disruptive students
laugh at me, with disdain challenge me and the Word. They prefer to
talk of socialism, spells and witch doctors who they say can heal folk
and can predict the rains from scattering a bag of bones across the floor!
I ask you. So though I am not yet of wavering faith, I am certainly of
clouded vision and drifting hope, feel that I have failed in my mission
for God, am no good at it. I wonder if I have saved a single soul.
The stress of it is showing: my face in the mirror is like a sodden pie
and I have got the doctor to give me some pills. I see the Principal
once a week to discuss my fears. He says my work is valued. Pray for me.

...

Worrying times now. Our work for God in the college is under
threat with millions cut from capital expenditure, ostensibly for economy.
But rumour is that the real reason is political, they can't tolerate our
independent work going unchecked. All this smacks of true dictatorship.
But Europeans are safe for many years yet because, frankly, they can't

manage without experts of the kind we supply. Could they, our situation would be rather poor. Similarly with the Churches. At the moment they are indispensable because they run the whole educational system, but if they could be dispensed with…!! Do not misunderstand me, there is no anti-European feeling among the mass of the people for neither Africans nor the Europeans like the look of the present Government. I hope that Spring has come in England and banished all your winter pains and worries – not least the fuel problem. No such problem here: we bake and pray that the Harmattan wind is on time this year to cool our sleepless nights.

...

Father, my work here will soon be over: at the ordination of a colleague three ministers stood behind him, then came the imposition of hands. Four black hands and two white were placed on his head. It told me something. That the work of God is now with them. So I have spoken to London and my boss here and it is decided. Altogether, I am rather glad that I'm leaving to return to work in England. The total atmosphere is not good, particularly when I compare it to what things were like on my first tour when I felt wanted and His work felt wanted. But now? I look forward to seeing how your garden is growing. We have had a good many tomatoes but nothing much else because of poor seed. I will let you know when it is finalised that I leave. I'll probably fly and put things collected on the boat – ivories, beautiful tribal wooden carvings, masks, drums. Some are hundreds of years old and should fetch a good price. It's settled I'll get a circuit at Kidsgrove – though plan to write for His Kingdom Overseas too. Blessings.

Oranges

I had them again last night,
thick-skinned and glowing,
tumbling fast towards me
from a great blue height –
thousands, rolling over and over,
jostling in rumbling jumble.
I reached out, caught,
took my thumbnail, jagged
deep into the small green eye,
felt the sting in a tiny graze.
I peeled slowly, tore back
heavy skin to reveal
an old man's head, sore,
wispy hairs quivering
like feelers in the breeze.
Now exposed,
I began to squeeze it,
to rub, cover my arms, thighs
with juice, seed, pulp
until I shone brightly,
a burnished copper figure –
then held my finger high
to drop that last trickle
onto my tongue, gulped down,
the tang holding my jaw
in a wide, tight embrace
for each segment,
flesh surrendered.
I ate them all
as they came.

This morning, for what
and for whatever reason,
they pelt me with doubt,
full in the face, like
a lover in a quiet moment
with a what are you thinking
about now. And, as usual,
the sky is guilt-grey, sunless.

What Did You Do Today?

It's hard to take if you like to look.
And she had looked at the wall
for most of the afternoon,
letting the idea form its centre,
waiting for it to give, a word,
a phrase, a line – one little ball
grows bigger and bigger and bigger.
And with it she had found
the locus of her senses -
the smell of graphite,
the stories she had written
as a girl. Free, unhindered, often.
So she laid out pencil and paper.
She would start tomorrow.
No time now: soon
he would be home with

What did you do today?
Explaining has no capital –
this much she had accumulated
over twelve years, so,
as usual, she hurdled the question
with a list of chores, took
his briefcase, put it in its place:
then she watched him eat. Her food.
His food he said.

What did you... today
he microwaves his own dinner,
phones around for answers.
But today she has taken the first step,
watches the first words appear,
the beginnings of a script
for a documentary about a woman
who disappears, apparently
for no reason. She smiles. Yes,
she will make them feel sorry
for the husband. Make the woman
the guilty one. No, she thinks,
this is fiction. Or a play.
Or she could make it
that there is no one else involved,
whatever anyone might think.
Everything begins to flow
as her swaying hand takes

to the train's rhythm,
as her eye adjusts
to the look of distance,
to the appearance of something done.

Going Home
I.

The sort of family where no one hugged
(though we had a cousin who lived down south
and had seen him kiss his mother once),
where love was silent, emotions
mostly bottled, tears kept for funerals.
And you rarely talked about anything close,

like how he had got the hump on his spine.
It came out chipped away in bits through years:
the bike; the hill; the brakes; the wall; the months
flat out in plaster head to toe, the age
of convalescence by the Southport coast
where from a girl she had worked in service,
already arched by sinks to low and floors
('it's all there was and they fed you well').
There, hands first curved together and the edge
of the sea was as far as the future:

the years of having us. Us who visit
when we want now we're just a drive away
to mow the summer grass and to bring more
children's photos to fill the bureau top. And
they fill the kids with stories we should have known
to draw us closer years ago. Too late,

as if one of them has got to go
before you begin to think. Inside, you try
to get time back through things you could have said.
Outside, we watch her back, bent as a sheet
just through the mangle ('the automatic doesn't
get the whites quite right'), bent as the shape
of every Monday, bent as the winter arc of sun
on a shortening afternoon, bent as her stoop
to give the final kiss: speechless.

II.

If you think that you're losing yours
even if in just more wherezthekeys days
or Nelson Mandela is whatsizname
and Stoke is wheredyamacallit,
you'll know how hard it gets to live
in a world endowed with – or rather
burdened with memory – or find it
so hard to believe a forgetting of this life
could be so difficult – this getting out
of this place towards the end – this place
I mean where I lived as a child and youth
and where we alive in those years have left
things – relics of ourselves – like the house
for sale they thought that seeing again
would reset the pain of my forgetting
a grandchild's name – as if fresh sight
of that path long enough for a decent run-up
or the webby worn grey carpet on the stairs
would revive the cells – or when they said that
at an upstairs window I'd seen the setting sun
as a big red six-hit cricket ball balanced
on top of the tree I'd climbed they thrilled
so got me this marblette notebook to put it down
to restore myself – like how their arboretum
I saw still as our over-grazed paddock where
only thistles thrived with stems tense with strength
and by moonlight spikes sheened silvery green
under purple plumes flaring blue like jets of gas
– how the bedroom had reminded me
of sitting with our hacking Joe and deciding only
two colours mattered – the yellow in his face
and the red of gobfuls he spat into the jerry
by his bed – yellow and red to warn us for sure
of his tragedy in store and be watchful of when
it would fall – how the memory of such stuff
now makes me more struck by the way
I remain just as I always was than by the way
I've evolved into what they see me as or
fear I am – makes me sure I still have a grip
gently easing out what hides with this soft pencil
unravelling and guiding the lines from was to is.

Henry Whiston

filled the chapel with fellow miners
and scent from his favourite roses
covering the coffin lid, white
as his wife's dabbing hankie.

Numb in an untrue eulogy, I wondered
if they'd sewn his legs back on
if that cutter was mended yet
and the official inquiry finished.

They shouldered him out in rain.
We followed, saw bearers slipping a bit
on the mossy blue brick path
lined with villagers bowed in respect.

Then at the lowering in, his best mate Joe
howled like Beech's dog the day it bit me,
sobs drowning out the minister's drone.
And me forever changed at that sight

of a man crying at the death of another man,
at what I'd been taught was not allowed.
Where was that rule, the *manly* silence of death
that's supposed to dignify and terrify us?

All I knew was that I saw for the first time
a man I knew behaving how he felt,
not weak, not showing what death is like
but what life is like, his love is like.

Opened by something that had happened,
touched by something new, didn't know of,
something I couldn't control
killing what they'd told me to be like,

something was now saying
don't be frightened of what you feel.
Walking home, I felt alive with it,
wanted to tell of it. But in a waft of baking,

mother only wanted to know who was there,
if he'd had a good turn out and said
her potato scones would be cooled in time
for me to take for snap on the night shift bus.

I Crave A Listener For This

Mother always had trouble with *absence:*
was there a *c* after the *s*?
And *what shall I say this time?*
in the dreaded note for school
after another dose of bronchitis.
Or to excuse me from games
because of a bout of wheezing.

I picture her in a state of helplessness,
Bic biro poised over the lined pad
of Basildon Bond, tormented yet again
by what to put, by what they'd think
of her writing, by guilt for bringing us up
among damp walls and smoking kilns.
And worry-worn that choices killed
by every childhood illness choked off
getting on, a competing for certain prizes:
results are affected by his absences
wrote Mr Webb in his third-year report.

And I write in a helplessness,
tormented that the right words
did not claim me in time to tell her,
she had no blame for the dealt hand,
of her love as the greatest prize I hold.

Part III

Potters: A Division Of Labour

A sequence for the workers of the Alfred Meakin Pottery, Tunstall, Stoke-on-Trent, 1964

Preface

Biddulph Moor. Half past seven. I'm waiting with Mary Mellor at the bottom of Hot Lane in a cold, damp early morning mist. 'He gives rain', says Mary referring to the wireless weather forecaster. She tightens the knot of her headscarf under her chin and stamps her feet. It is the end of June. I shiver, mostly with nervous expectation at the prospect of my first job. I've got a university place and just done my A-levels but my dad says that just in case I don't get them I've got to think about getting a job, to 'bring something in' anyway. A wage. Ralph Brown, the captain of our youth club football team, works as a placer at the Alfred Meakin Pottery in Tunstall and has got me a start as a mould runner. No interview, I haven't got a clue what the job is or what I'll be doing. We are waiting for Ralph.

Suddenly his Hillman Husky coughs its way out of the fog. Gasping through the clouds of choke-out exhaust fumes, we squeeze in. We stop to fill up in the village at Billy Booth's garage. A copy of yesterday's *Evening Sentinel* is on the dashboard. I scan the headlines and when he gets back in, I ask if I can have it to read at dinner time: it goes in my duffel bag with the packed lunch. It would be great to tell you I kept that paper – and I can. Somehow it went into a box with old Port Vale and Stoke programmes and browning copies of the *Biddulph Chronicle* that my mother hung onto whenever there was mention of us or the chapel or her Women's Institute.

So I can tell you that along with my own momentous step into another world, the world was turning momentously. On the front page, next to a photo of Princess Margaret arriving at Stoke station for the degree ceremony at Keele University where she's Chancellor, there's a piece on the television strike with 3500 out and Wimbledon the first to be hit: and no Coronation Street. Beneath, there is the Russian spacecraft launch, a rebellion in the Congo, African leaders call for action in Rhodesia and Nelson Mandela is jailed. On the inside pages, Malcolm X has flown into London warning that 'a bloodbath is on its way in America': the Civil Rights Bill has been signed but an Atlanta restaurant owner says he would rather go to jail than integrate. At home, the Great Train Robbers have gone on trial, police leave has been cancelled as The Beatles go home to Liverpool and there are more strikes – Ford's Halewood plant is at a standstill, 5000 post office workers walk out in London. Closer to home, there's to be a new police headquarters in Hanley, a new £19 million plant at Shelton iron and steelworks, a new shaft has been sunk at Florence Colliery though 800 a week are leaving the mining industry and there's been a £1 million jump in the value of pottery sent abroad.

Political Commentary by 'Radar' is predicting an October election. June has been 'sunless' which might have made the job adverts for 'make your home in Canada' and shunters on South African Railways worth considering. Or to cheer you up locally you could go to see Gary Sobers playing cricket for Norton, Wes Hall for Chell or watch Staffordshire beating Norfolk in the Minor Counties League. Elsewhere in local sport, John Ritchie is refusing to sign terms with Stoke City and at Vale Park, manager Freddie Steele is having similar problems with John

Nicholson and Stan Steele. If you want to go out, traditional jazz and rock/pop groups are clashing: The Place in Hanley is the in place with Georgie Fame, The Crickets, Long John Baldry, Victor Brox ('with sensational coloured vocalists'!) or you can catch The Who or Them at the Harold Clowes Hall or Dr Who and The Daleks in a pub in Hanford. The George Hotel in Burslem has the Red River Jazzmen and the Savannah Jazzmen against The Ceramic City Stompers at The Crown & Anchor in Longton – and 'adult dancing' thrives at the Crystal Ballroom. Though there's a report of a Congleton cinema switching to bingo, there's wide choice elsewhere in the Potteries including *Tom Jones, Carry On Jack, Cleopatra* and Brigitte Bardot in *Please Not Now (X)* ! No such scandal at the Victoria Theatre where they're doing *The Dock Brief* and *A Night To Make The Angels Weep* for those who don't fancy the wrestling at the Victoria Hall where Jackie (Mr TV) Pallo is taking on Count Bartelli.

If you've not booked your holidays, there is still full board in Blackpool for £1 a day or if you're staying at home you can prepare for winter at Huntbach's sale with Chilprufe Vests and Vantona Bedspreads or, if you want to get out of town for good, buy yourself a semi-detached bungalow at Loggerheads for £2340.

But reading that *Sentinel* again, it is the Situations Vacant section that still stamps the memory most powerfully: Biscuit Placer, Gold Stamper, Mouldmaker, Glost White Selecter, Gold Scourer, Mould Runner, Clay Carrier, Scrap Carrier, Night Sweeper, Lithographers, Transferers, Turners for Red Teapots… All wanted. It became the trigger for the idea for what follows in the rest of this book. As the Hillman chugged up Furlong Road, turned onto the A50 then left to park on Parsonage Street and with the walk under the carriageway arch with Ralph and Mary, that was the world I was about to enter.

And writing this it seems too that I was entering the world of Edwin Clayhanger, just having left school, wondering what the future held, with that *puzzling world and the advance guard of its problems bearing down on him.* [1] At the same time I was Edwin's father: *Darius began his career in earnest. He was 'mould-runner'…* ' And so that world became a poem.

---

[1] from *Clayhanger,* Arnold Bennett, Methuen, 1910

Rex, The Dish Maker

The iron template is lowered slowly
to shape the piece of clay
newly splat
upon the plaster mould.
Then the maker's eye
and arm of years
create a Doric tray.
And in the spinning wheel
glazed eyes imagine
the pot's four-star destination
or recall the caravan at Rhyl.
For no rush
to meet the export order:
Rex is staff.

Chris, The Plate Maker

Piecework Chris
thinks in dozens,
cools off at dinner time
in Tunstall baths
and floating dreams
of Annie the Sponger.

In the afternoon,
another five dozens
will buy

the engagement ring.

Doris, The Cup Handler

The six-foot lump with hands like spades
deftly joins up cup and handle

as only seconds slip
into eight hours

of joining up cups and handles
with endless fags and talk

of bingo, television
and sex,

yelling down the shop
to the blushing young under-manager,

'Come 'ere and let me see
if your rhubarb wants pullin'!'

Terry, The Mould Runner

Not all there
and always late,

all day
he carried the moulds

in and out of ovens
with no time to by-pass

the unpleasantness
of one hundred degrees

until the day he stopped
to tell the world,

'The clay is dead,
the clay is dead.'

Hilda, The Fettler

For fifty years, she filed
or, as we say, fettled,

rough edges to dust
from unfired pots

until each lung became
a piece of clay

so that when she retired
they could present her

with an unremitting cough.

Frank, The Manager

White coat
with built-in biros
ticks off latecomers,
ticks clipboard,
cheerios and
blind to V-signs,
microscopes clock cards
looking for seconds
each the width
of a grey hair,
the thickness
of a pound note,
the dimension
of his own life.

Barry, The Clay Carrier

Perfumed, hair dyed black
as his shiny winkle-picker shoes
taunts of 'puff' are silenced
by cutting the longest slug of clay
from the pug machine's conveyor
rollers, sliding it up his thigh
then flipping it effortlessly
over his shoulder like a lover's
gaberdine. Nonchalantly he cracks,
'Not bad for a nancy boy then, eh?'
Then under his burden he ponces
down the yard without a stagger
to keep his piece-work maker fed
singing Shirley Bassey numbers
all the way, rehearsing his repertoire
and working out his outfit
whether or not to wear stilettoes
for the open mike that night
at Cobridge British Legion.

Johnny, The Placer

Silent whether drawing down
a fired kiln not cooled enough
or stacking saggars
the other placers knew
that even in his glide
across the dusty yard
with a board full of jugs
balanced on his padded cap
that he was somewhere else
either batting at three for Chell
or darting for The Goose.
Some weeks it seemed like
he only ever spoke on Monday
if the Vale had won
and Stoke had lost.
For this was Tunstall.

Eric, The Plate Maker

Fastest in the place
robot-like he loads
the automatic jig
with no time to joke
about piles or cucumbers
unlock the muteness
in case he loses a piece
slackens the pace.
Some say he gets
the potbank's biggest wage
is money-mad and
that one day he'll drop.

Others say he's simply under
the thumb of a wife
who wants to buy
an oatcake shop.

Joe, The Director

The big black Alvis
is parked for the meeting
not long enough
for soot to settle
on the shiny bonnet.
Inside, leather and walnut
wait silently for the decision.

In the mahogany boardroom
they hear that orders are down
and profits cut but vote
to give a dividend on shares.
But no rises for the staff.

Before the news has spread
he has slipped away
acknowledging no one but
worrying about the union's threat
his fat arse squirming
for comfort in the driver's seat.

Beryl, The Decorator

Only ever good at drawing
she could have gone full-time
to Burslem School of Art
but had to do with evening classes
for when her father went
they needed another wage.
Now she's in charge
of freehand painting
showing the younger girls
and telling them that in her time
she worked for Clarice Cliff
told them what it meant
to paunce designs. The colours
how they made her remember
the other girls when she dusted
the *Bizarre* pieces she'd kept
how once a dealer on the knocker
had tried to part her from them
when he saw the parlour cabinet
how she'd sent him packing
saying how to her they were priceless
pots, just pots which meant so much.

Alma, The Paintress

Third generation at Meakinses
from a grandad who couldn't read and write
and at it since leaving school herself
she's not so keen on the modern designs
all patterns of marks and shapes
prefers the birds and flowers and scenes
that Beryl trained her up on, the delicate
brushwork and care you needed. So
she's thought of packing it in but knows
she'd miss the praise and friendship.
And the new lines are easier so lately
she's speeded up which, now that David
has passed the eleven-plus, will help pay
for his uniform for Hanley High she'll get
from Huntbach's fancy shop up Hanley.
And as a present for doing so well
a Parker fountain pen from Webberley's.

Edith, The Transferer

Quick-fingered with the tissues
onto the ware, she likes her job

but moans about the ashtrays
and mucky jokes from the other girls

who call her a misery pot,
some putting it down to her Methodism,

the three times a Sunday to chapel
and not even touching a Babycham

or others to the three buses she's to catch
to work from bleak Biddulph Moor.

The shock of the lipstick that Monday
shut them all up. She isn't saying

but Doris says it's the new young minister.
Annie has heard that she's going

with a draughtsman from the English Electric
she met at the Crystal Ballroom.

Dick, The Mould Maker

Always in another place,
he hums through spirituals like
Just A Little While To Stay Here
cares for nothing but New Orleans
jazz, keeps his trumpet in The Roebuck
where at dinner time he blows
his blues in the deserted snug, fingers
coated with corpse-white plaster
crackling out solos by his favourites,
Bunk, Kid Howard and De De Pierce.
Sometimes he shapes the new, just
a phrase, a variation. Or simply tender
for loud. Walking back towards the din
he thinks that soon he might be good
enough to go to N.O., if he can save
and keep away from record shops.
And if his mother leaves him
the Wedgwood on the sideboard.

Vic, The Blunger

Officially 'sliphouse blunger charger'
feeding clay and water into the hopper
to make the slip, he sings on and off all day
above the churning racket, likes
to remind you that once he'd auditioned
for the big band at Trentham Gardens,
clocks off first to give his ears a rest
straight to the allotment's quiet
to trench some celery with a dad
still with trembles from Gallipoli
or, if it's pouring, for fried bacon butties
and mugs of tea from a primus in the shed
with Al Bowlly softly crooning *Nightfall*
on the wind-up gramophone.

Dennis, The Slip Caster

Forearms needled dense as newsprint,
blue-gowned, capped, surgeon-masked,
clamped corpse-white plaster moulds his patients,
bright lights guide fine motor skills
to sever halves apart to deliver new born ware:
oozed joint clay is scalpelled gently. So fettled,
trollied to kilns and paintresses, finally
his babies' glazes seduce gift shop buyers. And
he begins again his art of casting, feeding moulds
with liquid clay, what we call slip, pumped
from an umbilical tube on which his job depends:

till dinnertime. Then fagging in the smokers' lean-to,
he gazes out to low green hills on the edge of town,
dreams not of them or Ibiza with his mates
but the tattooist up Hanley who that night will,
with blood-red ink and surgical precision,
backstamp his unsunned arse with an arrowed heart.

John, The Student

They could teach him
a thing or two
like sending to ask
for a long stand
that the worry
of getting a woman pregnant
would get rid of his spots
that it was their taxes
which kept him at college
in drink and birds
that this was the best
education he'd get.
And he knew what they meant
would remember as well
how they listened
to what he said
when they asked him
what difference
a Labour Government
would make to their lives.

Brian, The Union Man

Choosing his moment
he would catch them
like in a warm break
when a high June sun
felt good on the yard steps
and persuade them to join
with the hope of better rates,
longer holidays, a safer place.
And the doubters who asked,
'Just what's in it for me?'
he would take aside
spread open his hands
and show them the dermatitis
ask how many they knew
wheezing away on the sick
with potter's rot.

Kath, The Office

Hilda told her that John liked books
so Friday when he came to get his wages

Anna Of The Five Towns was handy on her desk.
At his glance, she said Arnold Bennett

was a favourite, that she loved how
he described their people and places,

asked him if he'd like to borrow it. And John
coloured up, blurted that he shared her love.

Said yes.

John Lancaster was born and grew up on Biddulph Moor near Stoke-on-Trent. After Hanley High School and Sheffield University, he worked as a town and country planner, first in North Staffordshire, and then for housing associations. He played jazz trombone and started to write in New Orleans and Birmingham.

Since being a second prizewinner in the National Poetry Competition 1979, there have been five collections of poetry: *Effects Of War*, 1986, Giant Steps Press, *Split Shift* (with Geoff Hattersley), 1990, and *The Barman*, 1993, both with Smith/Doorstop; *Here In Scotland* (with Milan Knizak), 2000, Vetus Via, Brno; and *Potters: A Division Of Labour* 2017, Longmarsh Press, which won the inaugural Arnold Bennett Book Prize 2017 and is reissued here as part of this collection.

His work is widely published in anthologies, poetry and literary journals, including *Poetry Review, Ambit, The North, Times Literary Supplement, The Rialto, London Magazine, Encounter, Iron, The Alchemy Spoon, The Frogmore Papers.* He has held several posts as a writing tutor (Open College of the Arts; Huddersfield University, Workers' Educational Association) and his work has been used in educational course material (OCA, GCSE). He has performed work on BBC radio and television. He is former Chair, National Association of Writers in Education. He lives in Totnes, Devon.

Cover Design by Clayhanger Press
using image detail from
Biddulph Moor: oil on board
by Jack Simcock © The Artist's Estate.
https://jacksimcock.com/
Photo credit: The Potteries Museum & Art Gallery, Stoke-on-Trent.

Typesetting & Design Roger Bloor

Copy Editor Sara Levy
Proof Reader Adam Lampert

www.clayhangerpress.co.uk